Mama's Pearls

Sincerely,
Patricia Bee

Mama's Pearls

Poetry to Live By

PATRICIA BEE

To order additional copies of this book, contact:
Patricia Bee
P.O. Box 51
Beaufort, South Carolina 29901

17986-BEE

Dedication

Mama's Pearls is not an ordinary book of poetry; it is a manual for living. I honor my foreparents for the rich heritage that has been afforded me, and for the legacy that is being passed on to save the next generation's seed.

I thank God for the opportunity to have carried the name, and for the wonderful proverbs that have given me strength for life's journey.

Oh, King Cotton

Cotton, Cotton
Who made you king?
For we were kings
In 'da Motherland

Now, you reign
But pain you bring
For we left our rings
In 'da Motherland

Tho' we bend
We will not bow
Tho' hard we work
Someday, somehow

No matter what life may bring
In 'da fields
We still sing
Freedom songs
From 'da Motherland!
Freedom songs
From 'da Motherland!

Young To Old

I've been young, and now I'm old
But I've never seen the righteous forsaken
O'er many miles, I have come
But never have my feet been shaken

I kept my hand in da' Master's hand
As I walked along the way
And I never took a single step
Before I knelt to pray

God calls the young, for dey are strong
The old, for we know da' way
Honor your father and mother
So that long may be your day

Psalm 37:25—I have been young, and now am old: yet have I not seen the righteous forsaken, nor his seed begging bread.

On Setting The Example

Children imitate their parents

From them, they do mock

And always remember . . .

Chips don't fall far from the block.

I Timothy 4:12—Let no man despise thy youth; but be thou an example of the believers, in word, in conversation, in charity, in spirit, in faith, in purity.

Sunday's Best

Mama got up early

For church, she got us dressed

Going to the house of the Lord

Dressed in our Sunday's best.

Mama cooked for the preacher

For this, she was blessed

Her work was done, as we dined

On our day of rest

Psalm 122:1- I was glad when they said unto me, Let us go into the house of the Lord.

Time and Tides

Time and Tides

Wait for no man

So child, take note

You do need a plan

The work that was started,

My God will complete

So, my child, take a stand

And do not drag your feet!

Joshua 1:8—This book of the law shall not depart out of
thy mouth: but thou shalt meditate therein day and night.

Grown People's Company

Stay out of grown people's company!

Mama said to me one day

'Cause little ears are listening

To repeat just what I say!

Proverb 4:1—My son attend unto my wisdom, and bow thine ear to my understanding.

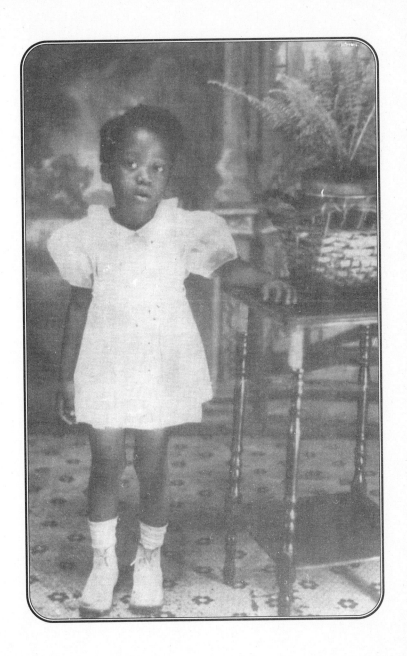

On Manners

Child, manners will take you farther

Than money will ever go . . .

The place you'll find your blessings

You may never know.

Proverbs 3:4- So shalt thou find favour and good understanding in the sight of God and man.

On Patience

Crawl Before You Walk

Child, you must crawl before you walk

And make sweet sounds before you talk

So only covet what's for you

For you will reap, when your season 's due

If in fact, you do not faint

A beautiful canvas God will paint

Of things that you could never dream

Tho' long the road your path may seem.

Galatians 6:9—And let us not be weary in well doing: for in due season we shall reap, if we faint not.

The Company That You Keep

Listen my children

Take heed to my words

A lesson can be learned

From a simple flock of birds.

Character is judged

By your walk, not your leap

Nor the words that you say

More by the company that you keep.

Amos 3:3—Can two walk together except they be agreed?

Half A Loaf

A half a loaf is better than none

I heard my Mama tell

For a man who don't provide for his house

Is worse than an infidel

So, if full time work, you cannot find

Take part time work instead

'Cause if a man don't do no work

Neither shall he be fed!

I Timothy 5:8—But if any provide not for his own, and especially for those of his own house, he hath denied the faith, and is worse than an infidel.

Think Twice

Think twice before you speak

Choose words before you let them out.

Others may get injured,

Hold your tongue, if in doubt!

Proverbs 21:23—Whoso keepeth his mouth and his tongue keepeth his soul from troubles.

Oxymoron

Bitter Sweet

Tho' these brogues
Are tattered and worn,
For my country I fought-
But my spirit is torn.

For women and children
I did fight . . . .
But sadly returned
No job in sight.

'Tis good to know
That God brought me back
But bitter sweet
'Cause my skin is black.

A Silver Tongue

Don't trust no man

With a silver tongue

Who'll promise you the moon

Or give you the sun

A silver tongue

Will you deceive

In him, my child

Do not believe!

Jeremiah 9:5—And they will deceive everyone his neighbor, and will not speak the truth: they have taught their tongue to speak lies, and weary themselves to commit iniquity.

Teeth and Tongue

Husbands, love your wives

As Christ loved the Church

Let the two walk together along da' path

Disagreements may come about

And teeth and tongue may fall out

Let not the sun go down on your wrath.

Romans 14:17-19—Let us therefore follow after the things which make for peace, and things wherewith one may edify another.

Concerning Security

My Grandma had a pension

From Papa she did draw

He left her, not like a drowning man

Grabbing for a straw.

II Corinthians 3:5—Not that we are sufficient of ourselves
to think anything as of ourselves; but our sufficiency is of
God.

When Company Comes

When company comes

'Tis no time to run

To push things out of da' way

For your house should be

Presentable

For clean your house should stay!

I Corinthians 14:40—Let all things be done decently and in order.

Concerning Friendship

Some people have two faces

In them you can't depend

For they talk on da' path

But walk in da' woods

Put not your trust, my friend!

Proverbs 18:24—A man that hath friends must shew himself friendly: and there is a friend that sticketh closer than a brother.

Double Standards

A man works

From sun to sun

But da' woman's work

Ain't never done!

Proverbs 31:15—She riseth also while it is yet night, and giveth meat to her household, and a portion to her maidens.

Concerning Work

Monday's Wash

Using a washboard

And a Number Three tub,
A 'squish', and a 'squash'
Many clothes Mama rubbed

With aching shoulders
In sunshine and rain
Clothes starched and ironed
Not one single stain

But if for her price
Others complained . . .
"Quantity or quality?"
Mama explained.

Jeremiah 22:29—Seest thou a man diligent in his business? He shall stand before kings.

Mama's Quilt

Mama worked all summer
Her patchwork quilts were sewn
From plaids, stripes, and polkadots
That all the children had worn.

We saw a piece of fabric
Taken from Aunt Ida's dress
A piece of clothing handed down
That could not fit the rest.

Mama's quilt was heavy
Every piece had words to say
Each one had a story to tell
Of how God made a way.

Lamentations 3: 22-23—It is of the Lord's mercies that
we are not consumed, because His compassion fails not.
They are new every morning. Great is thy faithfulness.

A Stomach Full

A stomach full, ain't but a stomach full

I heard my Grandma say

It don't matter if we eat pork' n beans

Just bless it when you pray

Thank the Lord for your bread

Who gave us seeds to sow

A stomach full, ain't but a stomach full

And nobody needs to know.

Phillipians 4:12—I know both how to be abased, and I know how to abound; everywhere and in all things I am instructed both to be full and to be hungry, both to abound and to suffer need.

When Da' Ship Comes In

My brother was da' sailor

My uncle was da' tailor

Both having wisdom

No doubt . . .

On their words

You can depend

Your ship will not come in

Unless you can be sure

You sent one out!

Galatians 6:7—Be not deceived; God is not mocked: for whatsoever a man soweth, that shall he also reap.

Strictly Business
(Peanut Man's Chant)

Parched Peanuts!

Pa- -arched Peanuts!

Grow'em in da shade . . .

Parch'em in da sun . . .

If you ain't

Got no money,

You can't git none!

Parched Peanuts!

Pa- -arched Peanuts!

Psalms 37:21- The wicked borroweth, and payeth not again: but the righteous showeth mercy, and giveth.

Nuthin' Wasted
(Lil Girls' Chant)

Ain't nuthin' like
Aunt Mary's 'tata poon'
'Tata poon'
'Tata poon'
Ain't nuthin' like
Aunt Mary's 'tata poon'
Made with orange peels!

Ain't nuthin' like
Mama's bread puddin'
'Bread puddin'
"Bread puddin'
Ain't nuthin' like
Mama's bread puddin'
Made from day old bread!

Ain't nuthin' like
Mama's hot biscuits
'Hot biscuits'
"Hot biscuits'
Ain't nuthin' like
Mama's hot biscuits
Made from clabbered milk!

Concerning Evil Doers

Fret not because of evil doers

They will be brought to the slaughter
Tho' they give for your good works
A sifter to carry water

Neither be thou envious
Against the workers of iniquity
For if you wait upon the Lord
He will surely honor thee

You must love your enemies
Do good, but do not fret
For the thing that God has promised you
You will surely get.

Psalm 37: Fret not thyself because of evil doers, neither
be thou envious against workers of iniquity.

On Revenge

Grandma said . . .

Every cat has its afternoon

Every dog has its day

Vengeance is mine,

Saith the Lord

And I will repay.

(Hebrews 10:30—For we know Him that hath said, Vengeance belongeth unto me, I will recompense saith the Lord.)

The Bridge

Remember the bridge that took you

For you may come again

Every day won't be sunny

Some days will have rain.

Remember the bridge that took you

And don't pull up the plank

For it was this very bridge

That launched you from the bank.

(Psalm 103:2—Bless the Lord, O my soul, and forget not all His benefits.)

Concerning A New Employee

Old Rickety Bridge

Don't forget the old rickety bridge

That took you from the shore

A new broom sweeps very clean

And the old scratches the floor

Don't throw away the old for the new

But remember to make space

For the old knows every crevice and crack

When the new you must replace.

Proverbs 24:3—Through wisdom is an house built; and
by understanding it is esetablished.

Every Pot

On its own bottom,

Every pot must sit

To take pressure for a time,

My friend, you must commit

Tho' the heat intensifies

Tis' not the time to run

Every pot is responsible

To hear the words 'Well done!'

On Visiting

When relatives you visit

Please don't wear your welcome out

For they may not tell you

It's time to leave if you're in doubt.

See if you're imposing

From vibes on your first day

'Cause coming to see me . . . .

Ain't like coming to stay.

(Proverbs 25:17—Withdraw thy foot from thy neighbor's
house lest he be weary of thee, and so hate thee.)

Watched Pot

My brother learned his lesson . . .

Years ago, when he forgot

To ask for a piece of chicken

And opened up Miss Daisy's pot!

So embarrassed Mama was,

When he lifted up that lid

If the floor could have opened,

There she would have slid!

And to this very moment,

My brother don't eat a lot

For that beatin' stuck with him

And manners, now he's got!

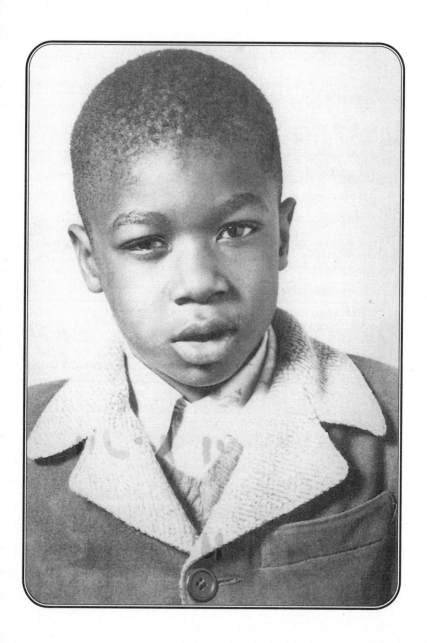

Try

I remembered Mama's words

When one day, I began to teach

A lesson that was new to some

One child, I tried to reach

"Words that begin with the prefix 'tri'

All have parts of three"

"Ronald, can you give me one?"

"Try and try again", said he.

I smiled and remembered

As I helped this child in need

"Try and try again, my child

If at first you don't suceed."

Your Best

When you have done your best,
You have done it all
Even if in the race
You stumble and you fall

Just get up
Keep moving on . . .
And, don't look back,
My friend

The race ain't for
The swift or fast
But he who
Makes it to 'da end!

Ecclesiastes 9:10—Whatever thy hand findeth to do, do it with thy might.

Excuses

Stop making vain excuses

Of what you can't do now . . .

For, If a horse you cannot find,

Go on and ride a cow!

Proverbs 19:15- Slothfulness casteth into a deep sleep: And an idle soul shall suffer hunger.

The Truth

Always be open

Consider what others think

Some may see what you don't see

Admit when your fish stinks

Barefoot Summer

Ain't nuthin like feelin'

Hot grains of sand
Sweet watermelon juice
Drippin' from your hand
In da' summertime!

Ain't nuthin like
Tomatoes from the vine
Sprinklin' salt 'n' peppa'
Feeling mighty fine
In da' summertime!

Ain't nuthin like
Drinkin' cold lemonade
Squeezed from lemons
That Mama made
Way down South
In da summertime!

Isaiah 16:9(b)—For the shouting for thy summer fruits
for thy harvest is fallen.

Candy Braids

A great big braid of candy,

My Aunt Carrie used to make

With my kinky, jet black hair,

So pictures, I could take

For a fit, I could throw

As I would try to flee,

But, my Mama's knees made space

And always captured me!

II Timothy 2:3—Thou therefore endure hardness as a
good soldier of Jesus Christ.

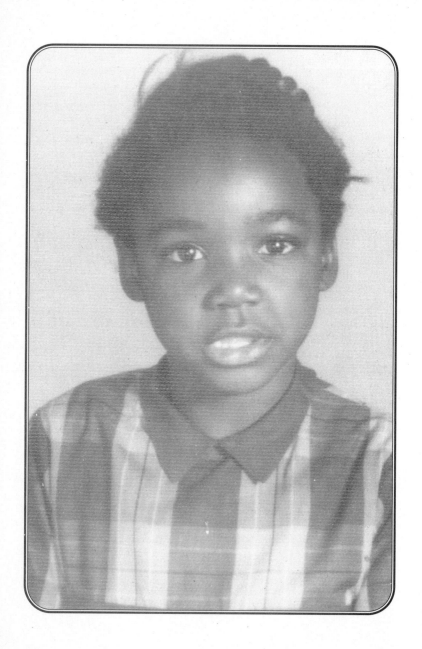

Black Beauty

A woman's hair is her beauty

I heard Mama say

Thick like lamb's wool

Was my hair

And it would not obey!

Ms. Julie tried to straighten it out

But, the hot comb made me cry . . .

Such a ruckus was raised that day . . .

She sent me home rough dried!

I Corinthians 11:15—But if a woman has long hair, it is a glory to her: for her hair is given her for a covering.

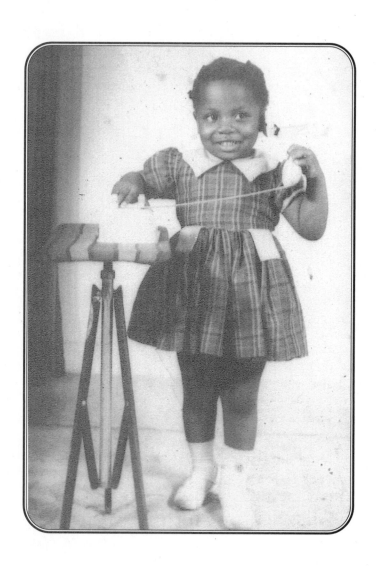

On Gossip

Study to be quiet,

Leave idle talk alone

'Cause ev'ry shut eye ain't asleep

And ev'ry good-bye ain't gone.

1 Thessalonians 4:11—And that ye study to be quiet, and to do you own business, and to work with your own hands, as we commanded you.

Knee Baby

Rock, little baby

In da' rocking chair

Life is so easy,

Without a single care

But, as you grow older

You will see

Your life will be filled

With responsibility.

I Corinthians 13:11—When I was a child, I spake as a child, I understood as a child, I thought as a child: But when I became a man, I put away childish things.

On Dependability

Broken Stick

Don't depend on a broken stick

It will surely let you down

Unstable is a double-minded man

So, why have him around?

James 1:8- A double-minded man is unstable in all his ways.

A Cat Will Eat Your Supper

Lil' baby boy,

You must earn your keep . . .

Rise up early

Not too much sleep

From dawn to dusk

In sun and heat

Work, so your supper,

Da' cat won't eat!

Proverbs 20:13—Love not sleep, lest thou come to poverty; open thine eyes, and thou shalt be satisfied with bread.

On Discipline

A lil' pup will lick your mouth

But a great big dog will bite

It's better to bend a little sap

Than a tree that's grown upright.

(Proverbs 22:6—Train up a child in the way he should go: and when he is old, he will not depart from it.)

On Confusion

In A Lion's Mouth

A kind word turns away wrath

So, rather than a shout

When your hand's in a lion's mouth

Be sure to ease it out!

(Proverbs 15:1—A soft answer turneth away wrath: But grievous words stir up anger.)

Home Training

Bend the tree when it is young

'Cause ev'ryone else can see

If at home, your child ain't been trained

And embarrassed you will be!

Proverbs 22:6—Train up a child in the way he should go;
and when he is old, he will not depart from it.

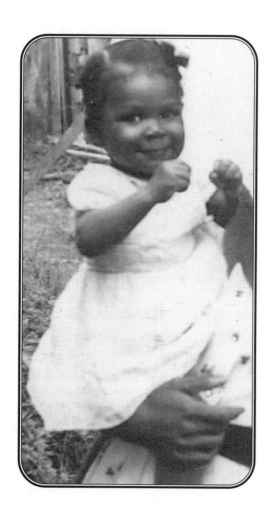

On Giving

Opened Hands

A closed hand gets nothing in . . .

Was one thing Mama said

She gave to those less fortunate

And never wanted bread

An opened hand is always there

To help others in need

For it is far more blessed to give

Than it is to receive.

Luke 6:38- Give, and it shall be given unto you: Good measure, pressed down, and shaken together, and running over, shall men give into your bosom

Sweet Dreams

Hush, lil' baby

Don't you cry
For you have sleep
Down in your eyes

It's time for you
To rest your head
To get washed up
And go to bed

To get you ready
For another day,
For you to romp,
And jump, and play!

Proverbs 3:24- When thou liest down thou shalt not be
afraid: Yea thou shalt lie down and thy sleep shall be sweet.

Family Tree

When Auntie

Was 'a courtin'

J.T. came 'a sportin'

When Mama asked, "Who might your people be?"

Tho' no formal learnin'

Mama was discernin'

A fruit don't fall

Too far from the tree.

On Chastity

My House Ain't No Hollow Log

My house ain't no hollow log

Mama said to me . . .

Anything can come and go

The snake, the worm, the flea

As you reach maturity

A lady, you must be

My house ain't no hollow log

So, walk respectably!

I Corinthians 6:18—Flee fornication.

Milk For Free

A man can wallow in the mud

And get up, still a man

But let the woman try the same

And she's counted as 'less than.'

So take this lesson in, my child,

Chaste, you must always be

For, a man won't buy a cow

If he can get da' milk for free!

II Corinthians 11:2— . . . that I may present you as a chaste virgin to Christ.

Caught In 'Da Net

When Jessie went off to 'da war

Dora began to roam

A fish done caught in his net

When Jessie got back home!

'Da child looks like Jessie, tho'

Since he began to feed

To disown 'da fish, cause 'e in da net . . . .

Child, there ain't no need!

Proverbs 6:32—But whoso committeth adultery with a woman lacketh understanding: he that doeth it destroyeth his own soul.

On Honor

Mama's Garden

We were taught to give our flowers

While Mama's eyes could see

She left us pearls of wisdom

To carry on our legacy.

Grandma's Stew

Mama says our family
Is just like Grandma's stew
Each has a unique flavor
Not the same of any two

Like the Vidalia onion,
Some of us are mild
Oftentimes, we're quiet
Occasionally, we smile

But like a clove of garlic,
Some of us are more distinct
When given an opportunity,
We say just what we think!

We all strive for excellence
We work while having fun
But like the ham or neck bone,
Some take longer to get done

Like the carrot or the pea
Some of us are sweet
It's because of this special blend,
That our family is complete.

On Trust

As a strong black woman,

Mama stood the tests of time
Working from dawn to dusk
Many days without a dime

Having to raise three children
Many times without a friend
She kept her trust in the Lord
To preserve her peace within

Maintaining her dignity
Came with a great price
Having to remain silent
Standing for her rights

She came this way by faith
Tho' the nights were very long
A diamond made by pressure,
The Lord kept Mama strong!

Proverbs 3:5—Trust in the Lord with all thine heart: and
lean not to thine own understanding.

A Gem

Tho' my Mama's

Dead and gone
Her words of wisdom
Still live on

But more than
The words she said
Was the Bible
That she read

Each and every single day,
Mama taught us all to pray
Mama showed us how to give, but
Her life taught us how to live!

Psalms 49:3—My mouth shall speak of wisdom: and the
meditation of my heart shall be of understanding.

Concerning Legacy

Mama was a Saint

Who used the word 'Ain't'
For, she only finished grade three

But her wisdom was better
Than those who had the letters
Of theology or philosophy

Mama's words live on
Even tho' she is now gone
In the lives of her children everyday

When I find myself in question
I think back on her lessons
And I ask myself,
What would Mama say?

Psalm 71:17-18—O God, thou hast taught me from my
youth: and hither to have I declared thy wondrous works.
Now also when I am old and gray headed, O God forsake
me not: until I have shewed thy strength unto this generation, and thy power to every one that is to come.

Strength for 'Da Journey

Every good road

Must come to an end

So must this book

You see

To your generation

Pass on da' legacy!

Acknowledgements

Mama's Pearls is a book of poetry that has been written to commemorate the heritage that has been passed down through generations of Gullah families throughout coastal South Carolina, Georgia, and Florida.

The wisdom of my grandmother, Mrs. Diannah Bee, was based solely on the Word of God. Though she only finished third grade, Mama was a genius; a lady way before her time. I honor my mother, Mrs. Delphine Singleton Bee, because it was she who carried me in the womb, bought me my first books, brought me treats from the laundry where she worked, and taught me to do my best. I honor my dad, Robert Bee, for teaching me to love poetry, for helping me to recite poems, and for frying hot, freshly caught fish. Thanks to Uncle Tim for sharing his turkey recipe, and to Aunt Ida for being the first in the family to graduate from college.

I honor my kindergarten teacher, Miss Katherine, who taught me how to write, and my first grade teacher, Mrs. Lee, who taught me how to read my first grade primer. I thank my third grade teacher, Miss Grayson, who taught me to go beyond the call of duty, as she sprinkled sawdust and cleaned her own room to meet her 'higher' standards.

A special word of thanks to my sister Rose, who called me daily when I felt the pangs of discouragement. To my brothers, for telling precious vignettes; giving sweet perfumes; To my sister Miriam, for sharing her Louisiana gumbo.

A special 'thank you' to my niece, N'kia, for encouraging me to publish this book, and to my nephews, to whom I'm known as 'Aunt Ann'.

I thank my first cousin, Brian, who took me to the beach, and reminded me of the stock from whence I'd come. Thank you, Victoria, for typing these words of wisdom, Connie for reading, and Ella for believing.

And finally, to the next generation, I entrust this legacy to you. For I could not keep it to myself, or allow these gems to be buried untapped. This is our God given inheritance, and for it, we give Him thanks!

Learn from it! Live by it! But most important, pass it on! And as you uncover these precious pearls, may your tongue be as the pen of a ready writer.

Birthmark

I wish I were a lighter shade
Of color, I did say…
"Gal, you're flyin in 'da Master's face!"
Mama said to me one day.

For God done cut the pattern
Ain't nothin' you can do!
Whether you are light or dark,
It's just another hue!

Smooth Black

Mama's skin was black

Black like the night

Her eyes were bright
Like pearls in twilight

Her hair was coarse
Coarse like wool

Her arms were strong
Strong like a bull's

Her feet stood firm
Firm like a mountain

Her hope ran free
Free like a fountain!

Jeremiah 17:7—Blessed is the man that trusteth in the Lord, and whose hope the Lord is.

About the Author

Patricia Bee is a native of Beaufort, South Carolina, where she has taught for thirteen years in the public school system. She is a graduate of Beaufort High School, holds a B.A. in Elementary Education from the University of South Carolina at Columbia, a Masters degree in Public Administration from Iowa State University, Ames, Iowa, and a two-year Bible training certificate from Rhema Bible Training Center, Broken Arrow, Oklahoma.